The Lobster and the Chicken

A Fable for Adults in Search of Enlightenment

by

Herb Palmer Jr.

iUniverse, Inc.
New York   Bloomington

iUniverse books may be ordered through booksellers or by contacting:

iUniverse
1663 Liberty Drive
Bloomington, IN 47403
www.iuniverse.com
1-800-Authors (1-800-288-4677)

Because of the dynamic nature of the Internet, any Web addresses or links contained in this book may have changed since publication and may no longer be valid. The views expressed in this work are solely those of the author and do not necessarily reflect the views of the publisher, and the publisher hereby disclaims any responsibility for them.

ISBN: 978-1-4401-2654-3 (sc)
ISBN: 978-1-4401-2655-0 (ebook)

Printed in the United States of America

iUniverse rev. date: 02/18/2009

Dedication

I dedicate this book to all of you out there with a dream in your heart. You know there is something better out there for you. You are in that $8.00 or $10.00 an hour job and you know there is more to life. You want to be free, not make your boss rich. I know you have heard this before. You have been to seminars and read lots of self-help books. You are not going to get rich quick, but the answers are out there if you keep looking. See your dream everyday in your mind's eye, feeling the feelings of that day and then believe-, really believe that you are worth it. That's it, you're on your way and the only way you can fail is if you give up.

I had the idea for this book working at a job I had outgrown. My boss is still there and some of the people I worked with are still there. The reason I'm free is I did something about it and I took action. Don't let that idea you have die, go for it and I will see you from the beach some day. So thank all the lessons, good and bad. They keep us moving on our path.

Illustrations by Dan Patierno
130 Ralston Avenue, South Orange, NJ 07039

Introduction

My name is Herb Palmer, Jr. and this is a lobster tale. This book is the marker on a 20-year path. I was awakened from walking sleep in and around the harmonic convergence in 1987. For those of you that don't know, it was a powerful planetary line up. The universe hit me with a God hammer and I woke up. That's another story and my first book, What you can't feel can kill you, tells that tale.

Several years ago, I was dating someone and in a deep conversation. We were talking about feelings, love, and intimacy. I discovered a character I have been playing in my life. I was introduced to my inner lobster.

Early in the morning as the sun wakes up, I see you on the water and I remember our talks. Thank you for your piece of my journey. I will always remember you, Misty

Nail. We are sitting on the sofa in her apartment having a deep talk about intimacy. She kept saying who are you, who are you. The thoughts that I had were of me and a boiling pot of water; I felt like I was being cooked. Because I had spent many summers with my family on the coast of Maine, I answered, ... "I'm a lobster." "You're a lobster?" "That's right?" and we both had a great laugh. I was all shelled up behind my feelings and not expressing my emotions.

And over the years, we talked about our journey. My favorite chicken would always run when the connection became too strong. The red high-top sneakers always allowed her to get away faster. So a few years passed. The idea of our journey somewhere in the back of my mind.

Then one day in the fall, a red tail hawk flew by to visit me. I saw her fly over the parking lot towards the woods. I have always been fascinated by hawks and eagles. My

Native American roots run deep into other life times. As I walked towards the woods, the hawk turned and flew back to me. She landed on a light pole about 30 feet above my head. What is the message, what is the message? There has to be a message. I sat there on the curb for about 30 minutes, just being with the hawk. No enlightenment or world vision, just a beautiful hawk on a warm fall day.

To take a step back, I was working at this job because of an intuition or a gut feeling. I had traveled to my sisters at the famous New Jersey shore. It was an unexpected week-end trip. The plans changed and I stayed there for a few days. I had another job at the time with big orange trucks, but that's also another story. I happened to look at the classifieds even though I was not looking for another job. I saw this great ad for a sales position. I decided to call ...just in case, about it. I started with them and because of the synchronicity I thought I would make my fortune there. I had just about forgotten my interesting reason for working there and my red tail hawk showed up.

A few weeks later I heard about a workshop by a Brazilian Shaman. Hawks, Shamans, they all fit together. That's where I met Alicia, who became a new friend. During our conversation I discovered she had a recent hawk visit. Driving through the Eagle Rock Reservation, a red tail hawk flew right in front of her car (her path). She stopped the car and the hawk turned back to look at her from a nearby tree. For me it was clear, the hawk energy was trying to make a connection. We stayed in touch and I had written the first draft of this manuscript. I felt I was guided or it had written itself almost as if the words were spoken in my ear as I was writing them.

In the book I was given the message to connect with the eagle and the bear. How do you do that living in the 21st century in New Jersey? There is a county park in this area that was a sacred place to the Native Americans. It's also a power grid that connects the vortex of the earth together. I told Alicia that maybe the hawk would show us the answer there.

We picked a day to travel to Pyramid Mountain. The night before, I received an email saying it. was a special planetary line up. I don't always understand this stuff; I just go with my inner voice. The message was your voice would be amplified a thousand times that day. The weather report was calling for rain, but that was the day. If our thoughts of love and healing the earth were amplified, that had to be the day, rain or no rain. I called Alicia and she was up for an adventure. So the next day we drove up there, put on our rain coats and walked into an adventure. I have been to this mountain many times in the past 20 years. That day, was like an invisible curtain had opened and I saw things that I have never seen before. By trusting our guidance and listening to each other's thoughts we found the bear and the eagle. Both in physical rocks that confirmed the writing in this story. I felt like a metaphysical Indiana Jones.

So now what, the hawk had led us to the eagle and the bear. What's the message and how do we get it to the world? Back in my office, a few weeks went by. I received the guidance that this book needs to be illustrated. I am a stick figure artist. I talked to a few people about any artist they knew. Nothing solid had turned up. I was talking with a lady I worked with. Ginger said a friend of her family is a talented artist. I called Danny and we met to discuss the characters. He had recently graduated from art school or cartoon college, as I like to call it. His specialty is lobster and has studied lobster anatomy. I felt the project was creating itself and I just had to stay opened and connect the dots. The first drawings are great. The ideas from my vision are captured from the air and he puts them on paper. So you see what I see.

Thank you Nadine and Jackie for your wise words and Cheri for your idea. I needed to know what chickens do when the lobsters go into their cave. Talking to herself and calling her girl friend was the perfect fit, thanks.

Next, I need to thank Lorraine for being my coach when I was stuck. Her book. Life touches life, is a powerful story of healing the loss of her daughter Victoria. God's plans are not always our plans; someday we will see the big picture.

Next I want to thank Barry Cohen my editor and friend. Timing is everything. He saw this book had something and that gave me the inspiration to keep going....

Thanks to George Joyce my business coach. He showed me the simple tools and training to create from infinite possibilties and get myself out of the way... To the lady that rocked my world form the day we met. Thank you Leslie Lobell, you turned me inside out and upside down. The lessons I learned will stay with me forever. I know what real love feels like now. It was great walking next to you on the road of life for awhile. I will never be the same lobster again..... Lastly to my family, friends and everyone that touched my life and put up with me over the years. If I was not looking out the window in school dreaming of purple cats, I would never have had the vision and imagination to my inner world that I see..... and thank you to the "circle of twelve" and the great white brotherhood for telling me this tale.........

Table of Contents

Chapter 1
Follow the Hawk

Once upon a time a long, long time ago in a place not too far from here called Hope, New Jersey lived a chicken. She grew up as an average chick. It seemed like a normal childhood; dolls, school, games, and dreaming of finding her handsome prince on his white horse. When she was little she had a feeling that she was special and had come to this place at this time for a reason. After seven years of marriage, a lot of self-help books and too much chocolate it was time for a change. So she quit her average job, left her average town, sold her 401K plan and started on the journey that would change her life.

One beautiful sunny spring day she went to find adventure and some how, some way discover who she was. As she looked up a red-tail hawk flew over her head. On this day she was not afraid; hawks and chickens have been feuding for years. The hawk seemed to be guiding her in a certain direction. She decided to trust herself and follow her guidance; after all, this is an adventure. Everything seemed as it should be. The woods and the small flowing streams were relaxing and comforting. The stress of her life had done its worst. As she looked down she smiled at her red high top sneakers. She bought them a few years back for protection. They were less of a fashion statement and more for defense. Every time since she was a chick the same thing happened. Dating and relationships had always been a challenge. Everything seemed perfect in the beginning, and then the power struggle would begin. He would want this and she wanted that. It always seemed impossible to resolve. Years of the same pattern with different partners, and it always ended the same. They would fight and she would leave. The chicken learned to run away and avoid conflict. After a big fight with an old boyfriend on Valentine's Day, she bought herself a pair of red high top sneakers. Now if she needed to escape they would allow her a fast get-away.

For many years the old sneakers were in her closet. The fights with her husband were never enough to run from. They always made up. Over the years, past resentment has built up. The fights lasted longer and they hurt more. Finally after another counseling session, she had the answer. To live the life she wanted the journey would begin. What seemed like an outer journey would become an inner journey.

Lost in her thoughts, she looked up--and right smack in the middle of her path was a huge old castle. Forbidding as it was, it seemed magical and intriguing. To go around the castle would be quite difficult so she approached with apprehensiveness. "Hello, is there anyone in there?"

"There's no one here, so go away," said a voice from inside.

"If there's no one there, then who are you?"

"It doesn't matter, go away."

"Who are you and why are you in there by yourself?"

"I'm busy guarding the castle from enemies."

"How do you know there are enemies?"

"Because they're outside the walls."

"How else do you know they are enemies?"

"Because they are not friends."

"So enemies are outside the walls and friends are inside the walls?"

"No."

"No what?"

"Why am I talking to you? You are outside the walls and must be an enemy."

"I will not hurt you; I thought you would go for a walk with me."

"Where?"

"Out there."

"If I go out there, and the enemies are out there, I'm not protected by the castle. I might get hurt."

"And what if you don't?"

"Don't get hurt or don't come out of the castle?"

"Yes."
"Yes what?"

"Just yes, yes, yes, yes. Yes to your life, yes to your freedom. Yes to your journey. Yes to facing your fear."

"You're confusing me."

"You can't be any more confused than you are sitting in that big castle all alone, watching the world go by out here."

"Maybe you're right; maybe there are answers out there, too--and who are you anyway?"

"That's why I'm on this journey and I intend to find out. Come with me and we will find out together."

The gate opens and the magical journey of the lobster and the chicken begins. As they start down the road 12-taxi cabs with all their baggage follow them.

Chapter 2
Cold as Ice

As they travel through the fields and small valleys they get better acquainted. The chicken describes her past life, as she calls it, and the conscious and subconscious choices that led up to now. The lobster mostly just listened. Even though he didn't plan this journey he sensed it would be good for him. For the past four hours the temperature had been dropping and the plants and trees had iced up. As they turned the next corner the sun disappeared behind a cloud and the cold wind felt like it went right through them. Then they saw them, the frozen figures that lined the road. Frozen with eyes wide open like giant snow ice cubes. The cave of the Ice Princess is just ahead.

"This is why I stay in the castle," commented the lobster.

"Don't worry, she has a message for me, I just know It," said the chicken.

As they reached the cave, more icy frozen figures lined the entrance. They slid down the icy frozen floor into the cave.

The Ice Princess rose from her throne and glared at them with looks that could kill.

The chicken bravely stepped forward, afraid but unwilling to back down.

"Why have you come here? I don't entertain guests," said the Ice Princess.

The chicken replied, "I'm on a quest for knowledge and a search for enlightenment."

"Why did you become the Ice Princess?" asked the chicken.

The Ice Princess responded, "No one has ever passed the ice forest that guards my palace. All that have come before you had fear in their hearts. The ice forest that protects me amplifies the fear and freezes everyone in their tracks. " "How is it that you are not frozen like the others, said the Ice Princess?"

The chicken answered.."I was afraid, but where I'm going is bigger then my fear of the unknown."

For a moment, there was a shift in the space, as the Ice Princess drew forward..."I was not born an ice princess. I was born a human girl into a normal family. My father divorced my mother when I was seven. My mother was never the same and became distant and unreachable. The more hurt she held onto, the colder and more distant she became. My father spent most of his time with his new family and didn't have time for me.

Sensing a slight touch of warmth, the chicken asked..."Did you have friends?"

The Ice Princess admitted...."I had friends when I was young. As I grew older I pushed people away. If I keep my distance I can't get hurt. I learned not to feel and my heart grew colder. One cold day my last boyfriend left me for someone else. I had a fight with my mother and that night she was killed in a car accident. That's the day I became the Ice Princess and no one until you has been close to me since."

The Chicken dared to approach...."So things happen for a reason. I'm not frozen because I faced my fears. You said your heart is freezing and you're going to die, so your answer is to forgive. Your choice is to die or to learn to forgive."

In a puff of breath, the Ice Princess confided...."I didn't know I had a choice. I thought the way things are is just the way they are. So forgiveness is a choice." The Ice Princess thought for a moment and said, "Everything I ever touched turned to ice. My heart is frozen and will stop soon. I don't have much time left. The answer you seek is forgiveness. I could never forgive and the more resentment I held the colder I became. Hurt and anger becomes colder if not released. If you can't forgive you will never be free. No one has ever escaped from my ice cave. If you bring this message to the world I will let you leave."

"I promise." Said the chicken.

One of the 12 taxis is left behind as a gift. The lobster started a fire in the taxi for the Ice Princess to warm up. The lobster gathered firewood and sticks for the fire in the taxi. The chicken arranged the sticks and wood as chickens do. The chicken helped the Ice

Princess light the fire. As the fire warmed the cave the ice started to melt. The warmth brought memories and feeling. When we remember, we feel and when we feel, we cannot stay frozen and start to live again. The lobster did not need a special message for himself; he gained enough wisdom from the lessons imparted to the chicken. It was much less painful that way.

As they left the Ice Princess and continued down the path, the temperature warmed up. A conversation developed about forgiveness.

"How can you forgive someone that hurts you?" asked the lobster. "What about an eye for an eye?" "You hurt me, I hurt you more."

As the chicken thought about the questions her first thought was that it's a choice. When someone hurts you, it is a choice you make to hurt them back. The chicken felt a cool chill move up her arms and spine like a message had been received. So there is a choice that's made at some level. We don't have to argue or fight--or kill at the most extreme; we choose to.

The conversation continued and the lobster and the chicken learned more about each other. How their thoughts worked and how they made the choices in their lives. The choices lead them to all their experiences, victories and defeats. With a choice there are consequences, even when you choose to do nothing, it's still a choice. The lobster learned to fight early in life. He was taught that winning is everything. Looking back at his choices he realized his walls kept him alone; protected, but still alone. The chicken also made choices; all choices have consequences. Conflicts and fights don't go away by avoiding them. They pile up until you can't avoid them any longer.

The chicken also learned early in life to avoid conflict and walk, or sometimes run away. All conflicts and arguments were swept under the rug. When the pile is big enough, you choose to clear out the dirt under the rug and find love and healing; it's all a choice.

Chapter 3
Army Ants

As they walked over the next hill they saw what looked like a battle. Smoke rising over the ridge.

Because of the elevation of the hill they were on they sat down and watched in disbelief. Seven armed divisions of the red army ants were fighting eight columns of the black army ants. Tanks and armored personnel carriers lined the valley as far as they could see. Bombs and explosions sent red and black ants in all directions. Burned out tanks and destroyed equipment lay about the hillside and valley. The battle raged on all day and into the night. The bombs grew silent and the lobster and chicken walked in silence down the hill as the full moon illuminated the carnage.

As they reached the road leading out of the valley, what they heard made them stop and think. Two crashed fighter planes smoking and on fire. A red and black army pilot, both mortally wounded, lay in a bomb crater talking. When they stopped fighting and started talking they figured out that they were not really different. They had kids about the same age and they all loved playing baseball. If they had met at the little league baseball field with their sons they may have been friends. So the question is why? Why have we been fighting for thousands of years? They both had the same answer. That's what we have always done. By needing to be right, we continue doing what we have always done. If we can never be wrong, we cannot grow and morph into our true selves.

The lobster and the chicken watched in amazement as they both died. Their souls left their bodies. As they ascended into heaven there was only one heaven. The difference between the red army heaven and the black army heaven was an illusion. If they are the same, why do they kill each other? All for the sake of profit to feed a destructive machine of fear. The purveyors of death become wealthy as our youth die. When people have peace within their own hearts, no one or nothing can force them to take a life. Indeed, the truth shall set you free. War, too, is a choice.

As the chicken and lobster walked in silence, the chicken was the first to speak. The conversation from the pilots reminds me of a story when I was young. We had meatloaf a lot. I asked my mother why she always cut the ends off the meatloaf. She thought about it for a minute and said, "That's what we have always done." I don't know, let's call grandma to ask her. Grandma said the reason she always cut the ends off was because it didn't fit in the pan.

How many times do we do the same things over and over again and never ask why? The path they were on became more rugged and the terrain harder to get through.

Chapter 4
The Writing on the Wall

They had reached the cave of the ancient lobsters. As they approached the cave, the lobster knew he must enter alone. Alone with his thoughts he moves deeper into the cave. He thought about when he was a little lobster, his father told him not to be fooled by the bait and get stuck in a lobster trap. Those thoughts were always in his head. Don't get trapped, don't get trapped, stay away. Without realizing it, those thoughts were the first stones in his castle. The castle was built thought-by-thought, stone by stone. One day he realized that the walls were so high no one could get in. Only now in the silence he realized that he could not get out either. Walls keep the enemy out, but trap those inside brick by brick, and stone by stone. By trying to be safe he had built his own giant lobster trap and didn't know it. He remembered all the times he walked by himself and didn't get close with others because they might hurt or trap him.

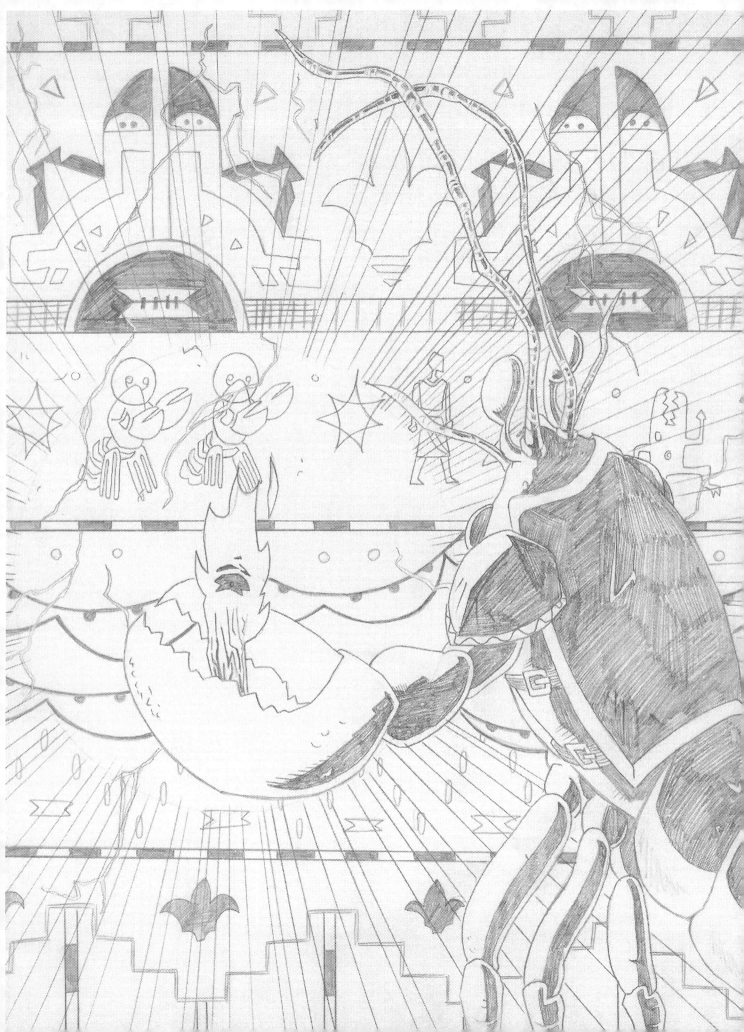

As he reached the bottom of the cave he saw the ancient lobsterian petroglyphs. These wise old ones knew the game. They started life on this planet long ago and left messages for the few who look for wisdom and truth. 26,000 years ago they had left messages coded into the stones and standing rocks for when the time would be right, and that time is now for all those who remember. There will be an awakening, a quickening of the spirit, and a gathering of all who have been asleep. They will remember who they are, why they're here at this time in this place and they will complete their mission. When enough have awakened, the vibratory door will open and all will remember and awaken. Many have returned for the final chapter. From a place deep within your soul, from a long list of lifetimes and lessons learned. The still small voice within grows louder. If you feel that chill run up your arms to remind you, welcome back. You have work to do my friends.

The reason it has taken so long to remember is your planet has been hijacked, so to speak. Other life forms with other intentions had arrived after the ancient ones left. Their idea for the planet was a slave race and a prison planet. They controlled through a thought range from a different dimension; because the inhabitants couldn't hear or see the intruders, they didn't know this had happened. The leaders had been pulled in through their emotions of fear, greed, anger and guilt. Once that had happened the controllers could do what they wanted with no one to challenge them, until now.

Back at the entrance to the cave the chicken had been as patient as she could; she waited and waited. Finally, she started talking to herself.

"Where is he? How could it take this long? What's going on in there? He must be somewhere else."

He still had not returned so she started talking to the cave entrance.

"Where are you? What's going on down there? Are you with another chicken?"

Finally about ready to pull out her feathers, she called her girl friend.

"I meet this great new lobster but now I can't reach him. He's gone into this cave and I don't know what he's thinking. He won't talk to me; it's like he's not even there."

Reassuringly, her friend replied, "You know how lobsters are. He will get back to you; it's just a phase. They all do that."

"I know, this one seemed different, I thought he really understood me."

After 40 hours the chicken had enough. How long could she wait? No one but an inconsiderate shellfish would do this to her. Finally, as she had made up her mind to leave, he returned.

"Why are you fixing your sneakers?" the lobster asked.

The chicken replied, "I'm out of here."

"Why are you leaving?" asked the lobster.

"You don't care about me; you left me alone for 40 hours," said the chicken.

"I had something to figure out and it's a long story."

"Can't we talk about it?"

"I thought we just did."

As they continued down the road ten taxis with their baggage followed them. The lobster looked back to the cave entrance. A space ship with two ancient lobsters beamed up a taxi with baggage.

This time on the path the chicken was far ahead. She was a little mad and a little sad. She didn't want to talk about it. The lobster's legs carried him as fast as they could. He was no match for the chicken and her red high top sneakers. She had become an expert at running away. Somehow this time was different and she could not bring herself to leave him in the dust. Somehow they had a message for each other. There was a reason their paths had crossed and this time it was going to be different. They both began to realize that if they understood themselves they would learn to understand each other better. She decided to give the lobster a chance. There must be a reason his castle was on her path. After all, things happen for a reason. She walked a little slower and the lobster caught up to her.

Chapter 5
To See from Above

They decided to stay on the path together. This part of the journey would lead them to the lost valley of communication. They were not sure exactly how to find the lost valley. Three hundred and sixty years had passed since the original people lived there. Somehow an inner voice guided them. They were learning to trust themselves and the voice grew louder. The original people who lived here were long gone; they had traveled away in search of excitement and riches. They had become lost and didn't remember where they had come from. The circle of life was returning them to the beginning. They seemed to be walking in circles. If only they had some direction or a map. The landscape seems the same; rocks, trees and corn plants. The original people could talk to the land

and the land would talk back. They had a sacred bond. From the time they left no one remembered how to talk with the land.

The original people had been given the message from the eagle and the bear. Since the original people had left the valley of communication, the wind was silent, the rain could not hear. The eagle and the bear had been in a long, long sleep. The land had been calling them, but they could not hear. The land was dying and unless the eagle and bear could awaken all would be lost.

Grandfather Sky had seen this all take place. His heart was heavy with sadness. He had dominion over the sky; the land and those on it made their own choices. They had free will. Finally he clapped his hands and the clouds crashed together. The thunder beings were hurling lightening at the land, in a last attempt to wake her.

The lightening hit a wise old oak tree that had stayed standing to remember the past. A branch burst into flames and fell to the ground. Instantly the four sacred elements of rain, wind, land and fire connected and remembered their sacred bond. They moved in the four directions to find the sleeping eagle and the sleeping bear.

The land shook and a rainbow formed in the sky. The eagle and the bear had awakened; the path to the rainbow leads to seven crystal caves. Only those with swords, shields and hearts balanced will find the caves. The messages of the ancients will be decoded there. The rainbow warriors will decode seven keys when they have passed their tests. 144,000 rainbow warriors will remember and return.

With the eagle and bear awake, a beacon is sent out. A frequency range only a seeker of truth can feel. The lobster is told to follow the bear; the chicken is told to follow the eagle. The lobster and the chicken continued on their path in complete frustration up and down through the hills, sometimes going in circles and doubling back.

They were both tired and frustrated.

"Why couldn't we find the valley? Why don't we understand each other?" asked the chicken.

"If only you could fly like the eagle we could see the valley from above," she sighed.

"If you had the strength of the bear and were not tired, we could go on and find the valley," the lobster argued.

They argued and argued and argued. Finally exhausted, they stopped and looked up; standing high on the mountain was the bear with his brother the eagle.

The lobster and the chicken decided to follow the eagle and the bear. They had to leave the road and the 10 taxis with their baggage for now. They climbed the rocks to the top. As they reached the summit together, the eagle and the bear were no longer visible. On the other side of the vista was the lost valley of communication. No one had been there since the beginning. The unspoiled beauty was breathtaking; plants, trees and flowers; purple, indigo, and crimson red. Why would anyone leave this paradise?

The only thing remaining from the eagle and the bear are two pairs of moccasins. The chicken took off her well-worn high top red sneakers. The moccasins fit perfectly. The lobster put his on and they fit perfectly. They walked for a long while without saying anything.

Somehow the moccasins connected them together to a deep inner wisdom. The connection allowed them to hear each other's thoughts and know why they had made their choices. If you can understand someone, walk a mile in their moccasins, so to speak, their choices and their way of life are easier to understand. Somehow fighting and arguing and making each other wrong didn't work anymore. They found an inner peace. A place to be totally honest and open with one's thoughts and communication here in this special place. In this place no one defended himself or herself. Everyone thought before they spoke and real communication was the norm, not the exception.

They walked back to the entrance to the valley holding hands. In this case holding claw and wing. Both had gained a part of the other and become something more with the message given; the lobster and the chicken started back to the road. They stepped out of their moccasins. The eagle and the bear returned. The guardians would stay until the energy of this valley could be felt all over the land. The time of the remembering had begun. Two taxis were left for the eagle and the bear. The bear roared and the eagle flew and the taxis turned into a new pine forest.

Chapter 6
Liquid Courage

The journey continued and nine taxis followed the chicken and the lobster down the road. The sun was right above their heads and the heat of the day was taking its toll on them. At the same time they saw the sign for Slimie's Clam Bar. They thought a cool drink was in order. In the Clam Bar were all types of clams; sad clams, and angry clams, big and little clams. The only clams they didn't see were happy clams. All the clams there seemed to think that all their troubles would go away at Slimie's.

The chicken sat down at the bar and ordered water. She started talking to the clams at the bar. Clam #1 always wanted to be a fisherman. That's what his father had done and his father before him. He had worked on his father's boat on weekends and all summer. When he finished school he bought his own boat. He had saved enough for a down payment and the bank financed the rest. For the first few years everything was fine. After years of fishing the bay had few fish left. He had to travel farther out into the ocean each year to catch fish. He seemed to work harder and harder just to get by. Then they raised the gas prices and that was it. He couldn't make the payments and the bank sold his boat. Now he spends some time repairing boats at the yard, but most of the time here at Slimies' thinking about what happened to his dream.

The chicken finished her water and ordered another. She learned a long time ago that she made bad decisions when she drank the wrong drink. The water was safe, cool and refreshing. She started talking to clam #2, who wanted to be a baseball star. He was an outstanding player in little league and school. He could throw the ball from center field all the way home. In his last year of school he was a super star. All the big schools wanted him. One night at the local drive-in movie, he made a choice. His son was born later that year. The only big lights he sees are the ones that light the highway for his night construction crew. He spends lots of time thinking about what should have been, and mostly trying to forget what is. Sometimes choices are unconscious. What are the consequences when you give up on your dreams? How many times are you going to get up after getting knocked down again? Do you allow circumstnaces to hold you down or are you more powerful than your circumstances? Choices and consequences, every day we choose.

The chicken moved over to clam #3. He always loved music. Ever since he was little he banged sticks or pencils on something. He played the drums better than anyone in his school. His band "Ghost Plane" started and was a popular local band for a few years. They mostly played cover songs. They wrote a few songs but never followed through on getting them recorded. It was always more of a party than a business. They never had any money left at the end of the month. After the lead singer moved to Hollywood to do soap commercials, the band broke up. Now the clam works at the music store thinking about what happened to his dream. When we tie our dreams to others' choices, those choices can affect our lives. Some people don't see or can't feel the car crashes and train wrecks they leave behind for other people to clean up. We are all one on this little green planet and our choices affect others. Again it comes down to choices; we can hurt others like we have been hurt or we can transmute that pain into love and healing.

The chicken finished her water. She had to find the little chicken's room. The lobster was nowhere to be found. While the chicken was talking with other clams, the lobster had a drink and then another. He soon had forgotten all his problems. He started to feel funny and his head started to spin. Then he started to see things; a pink elephant, and a purple rhino from his college days and a healing hippo named Joe. He lay down on the massage table for some energy work; as Joe the Healing Hippo worked on him, the source of the problem became clear.

Once Joe has centered himself, he connects to the land and the sky. Energy starts moving through his body and out of his hands into the lobster. He sees the protective body armor of a knight or warrior. The armor is from the past and is no longer needed for protection. The lobster was weighted down and unable to move forward in life. If battles no longer exist, then protection is not necessary. Joe removed all the parts used for protection in battle, and finally the armor chest plate that guarded his heart. The armor is piled onto the floor with past memories of battles fought.

As the lobster came back to full waking consciousness he opened his eyes. He felt lighter, like a weight has been taken off him. Joe said there are other ways to protect yourself; some use words and communication, others feelings, intuition and inner guidance. The lobster didn't know what inner guidance was. Joe reminded him about thinking the journey with the chicken was a good idea. As he remembered he felt a chill down his arms.

"That's your intuition talking" said Joe, "Trust it and it will increase. I want you to remember one more thing", said Joe the healing hippo. "The lessons that are the most important are the hardest to learn. Sometimes things are just the way they are. Hoping, wishing, dreaming and making them go another way is like swimming upstream in a raging river. You can only fight the natural forces for so long; even the strongest of warriors must learn to let go and go with the flow. If it's winter and you want it to be spring, it doesn't matter; it's still winter. Some things cannot be changed, no matter how much you want them to. You can accept things as they are or pretend they are something else. It's your choice; the second choice gives you no power. You then allow other people's choices to control your happiness and your life. This only leads to anger, resentment, more fear and loss of one's self."

The lobster walked back to the bar looking for the chicken. She was nowhere to be found. He talked to the bartender and ordered water this time. The bartender was busy reading the want ads and thinking about new ideas for his book. His book was called "Life Behind Bars" and was loosely based on his time bartending and his Uncle Fish. His uncle is doing seven years for armed crab robbery. He said his uncle is smart and he's studying to be a lawyer when he gets out--maybe even President some day.

The lobster walked outside and there sitting on one of the taxis was the chicken enjoying the day. They both learned some lessons at Slimie's and they left one of the taxis behind the bar as a gift for Joe the Healing Hippo. To their surprise, Joe had a whole fleet of taxis. Lots of seekers had been there before so Joe had more taxis than he could drive himself. Joe Hippo's Taxi Service was well known in those parts. As the lobster and chicken were about to leave with their eight taxis, Joe stopped them. Joe the Healing Hippo waves good-bye and the lobster and chicken start down the path again. As they talked about the adventures at Slimie's Clam Bar the sun was setting over the horizon.

Chapter 7
All That Glitters

They could see the lights of Sparkle City in the distance. The Glamour Queen lived in Sparkle City and all roads point to Sparkle City.

As they arrived in Sparkle City, the Glamour Queen drove by in her fancy sports car. She has the convertible top down and is the most beautiful white poodle the lobster has ever seen. Her beautiful fur and puffy white tail blow in the wind. Soon he starts running and the chicken cannot keep up. She sits down on a park bench and cries. The chicken has all these thoughts in her head.

"I'm not good enough." "Why doesn't he love me?"

"She's prettier than me" thought the chicken.

Puffie, the Glamour Queen, mesmerizes the lobster. He runs as fast as his little lobster legs can carry him. He goes to all the best stores in Sparkle City. Everything he could carry gets boxed up. Diamonds, gold chains, ruby bracelets and rings. The boxes were piled high over his head as he searched the city for Puffie.

He stayed in Sparkle City for 40 days. Every time he gave her gifts she wanted more, more, and more. Nothing was enough. She was never satisfied. He even took out a loan with an adjustable interest rate against his castle. The more it sparkled, the more it glittered, the more she wanted. Finally, having spent all his money, the lobster could not afford any more gifts; surely he had given enough to be loved. The Glamour Queen turned away and the lobster walked out of Sparkle City alone and very broke.

Well he wasn't really alone; three taxis followed him out of town. One left for the Glamour Queen. Of course she didn't want it because it wasn't new. He knew the taxi would gather dust on the side of the road in Sparkle City; maybe Puffie would find the old taxi someday. Several self-help books, a ticket for a special evening seminar and other stuff were left with the baggage. He had forgotten about his friend the chicken.

The other four taxis must have gone with her.

The chicken had awakened early this morning. Mist was evaporating from the dewy meadows as she thought back to that dreadful night in Glamour City. The time on the road alone had been good for her. After all, she started on this journey alone, so who needed that dumb lobster anyway?

The chicken said to herself, "If I love myself, it doesn't matter what anyone else thinks of me. If he runs for every fluffy tail, then he wasn't good for me anyway. What makes someone beautiful is much deeper than a reflection in the mirror."

Each time the chicken let her mind become still and become one with the silence, insight returned. She realized that when her mind chatter stopped, the information and insight that leads to wisdom is seen or, more importantly, becomes felt.

Chapter 8
I Wanted a Prince

The chicken was feeling the heat of the day; out of the corner of her eye she saw something green. Freddy the Friendly Frog was in mid leap and landed right in front of her.

The chicken shrieked, "You scared me. Didn't your mother ever tell you not to sneak up on folks?"

"I never knew my mother, she was not around when I grew up;" replied Freddy.

"So where are you going? Let's go out to lunch or dinner or breakfast even," Said Freddy.

"How about a movie or maybe a nice picnic basket?" he asked.

The chicken didn't know exactly where she was or really even where she was going.

"I have a long journey in front of me," commented the chicken. What would she want with a frog? He's certainly no shining prince on a white horse. But then, not every chicken gets a prince, does she?

Freddy said, "Let's be friends."

The chicken replied, "You seem like a nice frog, but I have things to do." The chicken, who really never understood love—real unconditional love—did not know that even frogs can turn into princes. Not everything is what it appears to be. When we love ourselves on all levels, we get to live our dream life. The chicken would someday learn that if you want a prince, then you have to love yourself enough to be a princess.

Freddy, not giving up, said, "Let's hang out, and let's be friends."

The frog continued to follow the chicken down the road.

"Want to go hang gliding? Let's be friends", said Freddy.

Freddy continued, "I've had a tough week, my pond is all dried up, there are no flies on my shelves and the Doppler radar says no rain in the forecast. So I'm up for a road trip, let's be friends."

The chicken replied, "Nothing against you Freddy, is that your name? I've been through this before and I only have time for me now, maybe someday, but not today."

Not giving up, Freddy said, "I know, how about roller skating? Let's be friends."

And so went the conversation, with the frog hopping from side-to-side following the chicken down the path. Every now and then he landed on her and she knocked him off with a good stiff elbow and said, "I said no, remember?"

They say if you meet a frog in your life, it's time to relax, clear off the mud or negative energy and sing the rain song. The raindrops are the tears of the sky and they clear whatever they touch. Maybe you just need a good cry to regroup?

The chicken thought and said, "My intuition is telling me to sing the rain song, do you know it?"

Freddy replied, "Any frog worth his weight in green knows the rain song. Ribbit, ribbit, ribbit."

The chicken said, "Ribbit"

"That's it, with feeling this time" encouraged Freddy.

"Ribbit, ribbit, ribbit, ribbit" sang the chicken.

Freddy said, "Can you feel it? I feel the rain."

Just then the sky grew dark and the sound of thunder cracked through the valley. The rain started and the frog was in his glory. He hopped from puddle to puddle, rolling and playing in the mud. The chicken sat under a weeping willow tree and started to cry. This time she didn't know the reason. Why didn't anyone love her? Instantly the voice inside her head replayed, because she didn't really love herself. There was always a sly fox here or a stray dog there, that wanted to use and abuse her. They all said they loved her, but their actions were always different then their words. Real love is unconditional, real love is a partnership. You can never find something that you don't already have within yourself. Her tears melted with the tears of the rain and stored up emotions, and finally she realized tears and emotions have to be brought to the surface for balance. When you hold something in and hold it in, finally it has to come out. It's usually not pretty. It's like carrying around an overflowing dumpster from the past. Every argument, the dumpster from the past always gets hauled out. When true communication occurs, the garbage is left in the landfill.

That's right, you did this and that and this; and oh yes, that. See here, it's right in my dumpster. If you want peace and harmony and communication, lose the dumpster. Remember we learned that in the Valley of Communication. She remembered the lobster had said something about rainbows or crystal caves. Lobsters, frogs, shamans; what ever happened to the Shining Prince on the white horse from her chicken hood?

Chapter 9
Tell Me a Secret

The chicken and frog walked by a small strip mall with a pizzeria and a fortune-teller. Madam Purrfect's purple neon sign flashed on and off as they approached. The frog pushed the bell on the counter. A sleek gray cat with a yellow turban and a red ruby parted the curtains. The frog sat patiently while the chicken went into the reading room.

Madam Purrfect asked, "What can I do for you my dear?"

"What's going to happen to me? I want to know my future", said the chicken.

Madam Purrfect sat looking into the large crystal ball. "Normally clients want money or relationship questions answered. When will my boyfriend do this or when will I win the lottery? You, my dear, seem different. You are a seeker. You want to know the future. What happened in the past?"

The chicken commented, "What does that matter and I can't remember anyway."

"You are creating your future from your past. Until you are at peace with the past, the future will not be as you wish." Said Madam Purrfect.

The friendly frog, who was listening by the curtains said, "What does that mean?" "I don't know," said the chicken as she huffed and puffed, losing some feathers. "I want

67

answers, not riddles". "I guess we have to keep looking," said the frog.

The chicken quickly said, "What do you mean, we?"

Down the road they went again. A taxi was left and installed on the roof for Madam Purrfect. They tied it with Christmas tree lights so all could see. The chicken didn't think Madam Purrfect deserved the gift. She did feel lighter with more baggage gone; lost in her thought she heard the now so familiar, let's be friends. And with a smile, she told him to get over himself. Three taxis followed them.

Chapter 10
Dark Places

The lobster's two taxis followed him. He was thinking about his time on the road and he missed the chicken, a little. That's funny "chicken little", but that's another story. He definitely felt lighter without his armor. He was a long way from the castle and it was easier to keep moving forward then to turn back. The lobster sat down on a log to rest; smoke began rising from under the log he was sitting on. Out of the smoke slithered a brown, tan and yellow snake. "Here, smoke some of this", said Smokie the snake. "You will feel better and forget your troubles." The lobster took a long puff, but never inhaled. He coughed and coughed and coughed. After the smoke cleared from his head he didn't feel any better. He told Smokie to go back under his log. What the snake said was a lie. The lobster didn't feel anything when he smoked.

The lobster finally understood if he couldn't feel, he was not really alive. This snake was dangerous and he would tell everyone he knew to avoid the low dark places in the land where the snakes lived. Stay in the light; avoid the darkness and some day the snakes would just go back to their planet.

In every other part of the journey a gift of their taxis was given in gratitude. Avoiding the snake and not doing what he said was this lesson. The right thing to do is still leave a gift. He dropped off the taxi, first at the body shop. They painted the yellow taxis black and white. The lobster put on red flashing lights and sent Flat Top over, who just graduated from the Police Academy. There was a small pond close to the log where Smokie the snake worked. Because there was a school of fish there, Smokie would do extra time in prison for doing business near a school.

Chapter 11
What's Happy?

The high puffy clouds were drifting by as the chicken and the friendly frog enjoyed the landscape on the path. As they crested the next hill, they heard lots of commotion. They walked into the woods to see what the noise was. A large tree fell to the ground and the chicken jumped out of the way; it just missed Freddy the frog.

Betty the busy beaver yelled "Sorry", as she scurried by. She was cutting down trees and brush for her dam. Three little ones followed close behind.

"I don't have time to talk. I have to take care of these little ones and I'm building a new house you see. So ask me your question so I can get back to work", said Betty the beaver.

The chicken asked, "Are you happy?"

"Happy? Happy? Happy? What's that?" "I don't have time to be happy. I have to do this and I have to do that. Oh yes, and then there's that again. Happy? Who has time for happy?" commented Betty.

The chicken walked away scratching her head. She started to think about her life and what was important to her. Could she balance her life so that happiness was a part of it? She thought about where the ingredients for her happiness were. Respect, kindness, love and communication; these were all important qualities to a balanced happy life. Her thoughts were shaken by the all familiar 'let's be friends'. To her surprise, Freddy was talking to the busy beaver. He decided to stay with Betty the Beaver as her pond was filling up with water. They are both water signs anyway and the chicken is an air sign.

That night they had a going away party with party hats and candles. The chicken gave Freddy the frog a taxi. He filled it with water and brought over some lily pads from the pond for a bed. The chicken gave the other taxi to the beaver. She quickly added some mud and built it into the dam. Everyone waved good-bye and the chicken was alone again on her path.

Chapter 12
If You Could be Me

Sometime after lunch, the chicken noticed a large crowd gathering up ahead. There seemed to be a long line of well-dressed classy chickens lined up to see someone or something. Maybe it was an audition for a part in a movie. Maybe discounts for a timeshare vacation. As the line inched closer, Rocky the Rock or "Rock" as he called himself was taking interviews. He has done several T.V. movies and a few shows in Hollyrock. The perfect rock specimen, bulging back and chest muscles, arms as big as beach balls. He normally didn't have time to meet chickens so he lined them up and from their interviews, picked the ones he liked. His perfect rock jaw line reminded her of that actor in the movies, "The Exterminator".

The chicken was busy fixing her feathers and applying lipstick as the line moved closer. The chicken started talking to a well dressed chicken in a business suit named Cindy.

"My cousin went out to dinner with Rock at his last filming of his movie", clucked Cindy.

"What is he like?"

"Well, he picked her up in a limo and they went out to a fabulous dinner," bawked Cindy.

"So what is he like?"

"Then he flew her to the beach in his helicopter to see the moon on the water."

"Sooooo....what is he really like?" crowed the chicken.

"I don't think she ever found out who he was, only what he had to show off with", cooed Cindy.

"So why do you want to meet him?"

"I don't know; that's a good question", Cindy answered.

She was next in line and overheard Rocky tell everyone all about his wonderful life and how great he was. His boat brought him here and his plane brought him there. It seems his ego went everywhere else. It didn't take her very long to realize that if Rocky was the center of his own life, there was not much room for anyone else. She laughed to herself as she stepped out of the line. All the hopeful other chickens moved up to take her spot. She laughed again when she saw Rocky's taxis and baggage lined up to the next county. The funniest thing was he couldn't see them. She left her last taxi for him as a gift. His ego and head were so big, soon he would need the taxis to help carry them around.

Chapter 13
It's Not My Day

The lobster was singing to himself, "Just say no", when his old taxi, now a Police car, went by. Smokie the snake was in the back. The law of Karma had put things back into balance. When you hurt another for personal gain, the wheel of Karma will turn to return what you have given out. It works for good stuff too.

Up ahead on the side of the road, a car had broken down. There was a long line of rubber giraffe necks slowing down traffic. It seems that Foxy had some car problems. She was in a panic. Kicking, screaming and crying at her car that had a flat tire. Even without her glittering jacket from Starlight Theater the lobster knew she was a drama queen. She was late for her meeting, as usual. Nothing was ever normal. There were always problems and drama; somehow she seemed to create them. Even when none existed before, the only thing that was always consistent in her troubles was her. She had moved to California--her troubles followed her; then she moved to Boston and her troubles followed her there. How did they always seem to know where she was?

When she entered a room, everyone always stopped to look, mostly because she was a half hour late and disturbed the back rows or tripped over her shoes. She always blamed things for this problem. The car broke, or I lost the directions or I ran out of toothpaste. Her excuses were longer than Santa's Christmas list. Because she was moving through life so quickly she never stopped to think. Never even slowed down to realize that it was not things that caused this. The reason was her internal guidance system (The wise ones called this the subconscious mind). Someday she thought that things would not make her late anymore. The only way that would happen was if she didn't go wherever she went. The lobster politely changed her tire. He decided he had enough problems by himself. He didn't have enough taxis to carry all the drama queen's bags.

He left the drama queen a taxi, but there was no way it could move. She had more baggage than the lobster and the chicken put together. Maybe she could use it as a display rack for her baggage.

Chapter 14
Let's Play Games

The chicken was enjoying the day and thinking back about her adventures so far. Every few miles there was a billboard sign for Gametown. Since she was going in that direction anyway, Gametown it was then. The sun was setting in the sky. What a great artist Grandfather Sky is. The purple and orange colors warmed her heart. She saw the lights of Gametown and all the glitter and sparkle of the rides. There were many games to choose from. She picked her favorite. "Try to get close to me and I'll run away." She spun the wheel and it always ended up the same. She spun again and again, always the same. The prize was always the same, half a stuffed heart.

By sheer luck or coincidence, the lobster was also on the road to Gametown. He saw the same purple and orange sky. All the billboards said the same things, "Have fun at Gametown." Many were already on the rides and eating cotton candy when the lobster arrived. He picked his favorite game, "No one can hurt me behind the walls." He spun the wheel and it always seemed to come up the same. He spun again and the same thing happened. The lobster prize was also always the same, half a stuffed heart. Dizzy from the spinning of the wheels, the lobster and the chicken each crawled off to find a place to rest.

The lobster and the chicken both awoke from the noise. It was early the next morning; Gametown was packing up and moving to a new town. The lobster and the chicken had fallen asleep, each overcome from playing their game again and again and again. The both of them walked through the empty field and watched the carnival pack up. Trucks and vans passed them by. They were both groggy from their dream. Their dreams were the same; they had forgotten and now remembered.

As they watched from above, they saw below them an old prison. An evil warden, set in his ways, ran this prison. Everything in this place was designed to punish and destroy the self worth of the prisoners. Every guard was the meanest, hardest guard in the system. You could not look them in the eyes. Every time you were reminded of how bad, worthless and what a loser you were. All the T.V. and radio programs had messages of hopelessness and worthlessness wherever you went in this place; you were alone and mentally separated from joy and self worth. One day after twenty or forty or a hundred or a thousand years, the warden went back to his own prison planet.

A new young warden was now in charge of the prison. Because the warden changed, the policy changed. Everything in the system changed. The old guards were replaced with enlightened, joyful and helpful guards. Each time a prisoner was around they were respected and helped as much as they could be. The negative T.V. and radio programs and newspapers that sold fear were replaced with only empowering, uplifting programs that taught valuable lessons.

All the negative beliefs faded away and the true self started to emerge in the prisoners. They were given more freedom to move around the grounds. At the final stage of the release program, everything had changed. The prison looked more like a college or a school for enlightenment than a place for punishment. The cell doors were never locked in this enlightenment center. The guards were all master teachers and the prisoners no longer prisoners but students. The doors were always open and the former prisoners, now students, were moving into the world. Now they are needed to teach, coach and spread enlightenment to the population. If they need to return again for a while for protection or a hot meal or to heal, that was fine. Then they returned to coach those who were ready to wake up and remember.

The lobster's prison was his castle, the warden was his fear. The chicken's prison was her broken heart and her warden was also her fear. They had the same dream, the same vision, the same fears kept them from love. Almost everyone is in prison, many never see the bars or the invisible guards. The warden is always our fear.

Chapter 15
High on a Mountain

They looked up and noticed each other.

The lobster said, "You!"

"You!" cried the chicken.

They both had mixed emotions. Should they hug each other or punch each other? They both looked down and they saw a shiny new penny. Because they had spent all their money playing games, they both jumped on it. He pulled this way and she resisted. As they wrestled for the penny a dust cloud formed. The penny was somehow more than just a penny. It connected them to prosperity and success. If they understood how money worked they would not fight over it, but that's another story. The dust cloud grew bigger from the fuss; it started to turn and twist. Soon it formed a funnel cloud and lifted them high into the air.

The lobster and the chicken merged together. Parts connected from the characters in the journey. Images from the Ice Princess to the Cave of the Ancient Lobster appeared in the twister. The lessons they learned were integrated into their beings. Fighting and struggling didn't work anymore. The more they resisted, the more the twisted persisted. The journey had triggered an awakening in the land. The Valley of Communication and the eagle and bear connected. A brilliant purple light shot from the land straight up through the twister. The frequency of the ancients has finally awakened. The purple beam carried the lobster and the chicken up, straight up through the funnel.

The wind slowed and they stepped out of the funnel at the top. Behold, The Ancient Temple of Crystal and Light.

Half way up the path a huge stone blocked their way. One hundred and forty-nine cedar trees guarded the path. A shining sword was encased in the stone. The lobster and the chicken tried to go around and over the stone. It seemed as though an invisible curtain blocked their way. The lobster tried to pull the sword from the stone; finally exhausted, he gave up. The chicken tried to remove the sword; she used all her strength; the sword did not move.

As the sun was setting, the shadows revealed the stone as the two faces of man. One side, the face of fear and the other side the face of love. The lobster remembered the message from the eagle and the bear. Through his journey he had balanced his sword, his shield and his heart. He centered himself and quieted his mind. He channeled the energy of the land through him; with all things in balance he removed the weight from the stone and carried it up the mountain. Because the huge stone was on his back, the chicken lead the way up the path. Together as one the task is completed. Talking to each other's minds they knew the exact location for the stone. The lobster returned the stone to the ground. Intuitively, as one they pulled the sword from the stone. Seven six-sided crystals on the handle of the sword started to glow violet. The violet ray entered the stone where the sword had been. The stone glowed and then split in two pieces. An enormous violet ray burst into the sky and four white whales emerged from the ray. The end of a 26,000-year cycle has begun and the violet ray fixed upon Mars the planet of war and his brother Aries the God of war. With all the power of the universe the four white whales pushed Mars and Aries into orbit. They would not return for a thousand years. Love was now the guiding force and fear would be a teacher in another place. The whales returned into the violet ray and the stone glowed and fused back together as a huge heart stone to remember this day.

On the path were the sacred stones that connected to the energy of the heart stone. This anchored the healing energy and reconnected them with the land. They both held a part of the stones; together in their hearts the connection was bonded. The lobster and the chicken walked by the glowing heart stone. It sank into the land to reconnect and anchor in the new frequency. The path continued up the hill and reached the steps of the temple of crystal and light. They walked up the steps. Huge crystal columns, like standing warriors, guarded this Holy place. Sitting in the center of the center, the heart of the heart, they see a wise old hermit crab. He represents the completion of a cycle. To get this far, the lobster and the chicken have reached a certain level of wisdom and understanding. Now they are willing to share that with others on the path. The hermit crab had shaved the top of his shell years ago. His long white beard shows he has arrived at the Summit of Understanding through a tough climb. He looks down at the snowy mountaintop. Very few seekers get this far--sometimes it can get lonely. He holds the lantern to light the path for all seekers.

The hermit crab shares with the lobster and the chicken the Laws of Karma and the natural cycles of birth and death. All is as it should be, no one is out of place and they have created what they need to learn at each crossroad in life. Only farther up the path does the lesson become clear. The hermit crab told them of the white brotherhood and the Council of Light. The twelve guardians of this galaxy. To their surprise, the lobster and the chicken learned they are part of the Council of Twelve. They needed to take their journey to remember who they are. Their job now is to go back and show the other ten how to awaken and remember.

The hermit crab dropped his glasses and the lobster and the chicken looked in amazement. The hermit crab had no eyes; he had mastered the art of seeing with his heart and his mind.

With a smile the hermit crab waved good-bye for now. When you finish your mission come back and we can have some tea and find time to go see that new movie "The Secret". There really are no secrets, just those who have spent the time to find them and those who are not yet looking.

The lobster and the chicken went back down the purple light. The twister started to slow down and return them to the ground. The lessons and the characters had turned to light and disappeared.

The lobster and the chicken looked deep into each other's eyes and remembered who they were. They both felt a tingling or a chill run up their bodies. The lobster's energy transformed and merged with the chicken's energy field. He now had some of the chicken's strengths, like running away from danger and logical common sense. The chicken had the same experience; her energy field was now protected by the presence of his energetic sword and shield. All she needed was to feel his strengh and angelic guards were at her side to keep her safe. The lobster had become a man, and a chicken at the same time. They had remembered their true selves. The chicken had become a woman, and a lobster also. She had completed her transformation and healed the past.

A light came down down from the clouds; when it disappeared two shirts were left. The shirts have the crest and colors of " The lobster and the chicken LLC" which stands for Lobster Loves Chicken. They are protected and guarded wherever they go. No one of this world can draw a sword against them without leaving the planet. For those that live by the sword shall die by the sword. Love is the answer now, everything else is illusion. The path they had taken led them to the ocean. A large Viking ship was waiting to take them to the next experience. There are three white dolphins swimming around waiting to guide them to Hawaii to uncover the secret teaching of huna. On the shore was a steam train going west. The chicken felt she needed to study in New Mexico with the native Americans at the four corners area.

Whatever they decided, the lobster knew the chicken would always be with him, even when they were apart. The chicken also knew she would always have the strength of the lobster; she just had to think of him and he would be there. It's your time now, find your chickens. Find your lobsters. And by doing so, you will find yourselves.

The lobster stood on the deck of the Viking ship as the steam train started. The whistle blew and puffs of hot steam flew into the air. He felt that some day the chicken would return and walk with him again. He knew all things happen in God's time and he was at peace with his choices and lessons learned. A large cloud of steam remained where the train had been. As the steam disappeared a beautiful white buffalo stood on the other side of the tracks. The white buffalo would bring peace and healing to the land and all of its creatures. As the sun shined through the clouds, he blinked and there she was. His beautiful friend, companion and soulmate, the chicken. As she walked toward him, she smiled.

"Sometimes us chickens can change our minds, you know...First we can go to Hawaii and then to New Mexico together and then to that place from a long time ago."

The lobster knew they were a powerful force for good together. All he could do was smile and remember their journey together. No words could describe the emotions he was feeling as three tears ran down his face. As she stood in front of him, they both knew they had found their home with each other.

They held hands or wing and claw and an invisible doorway opened. As they walked through the door, magically the chicken turned into a beautiful woman and the lobster into a handsome man. The journey was over, or has it just begun? It's your time now. Go forth and remember. Arise, and choose your destiny.